The 30 Minute Guide To
TRAINING YOUR COCKAPOO

By Simon James

Copyright and Trademarks - All rights reserved

No part of this e-book may be reproduced or transferred in any form or by any means, graphic, electronic, or mechanical, including photocopying, recording, taping, or by any information storage retrieval system, without the written permission of the author. This e-book is copyright © protected and is NOT free. You may NOT give it away! If you do, legal proceedings will be started for copyright infringement and compensation for potential loss of earnings. This publication is Copyright © 2015 by Simon James.

A catalogue record for this book is available from the British library. All products, publications, software and services mentioned and recommended in this publication are protected by trademarks. In such instance, all trademarks & copyright belong to the respective owners.

Disclaimer and Legal Notice

This product is not legal or accounting advice and should not be interpreted in that manner. You need to do your own due-diligence to determine if the content of this product is right for you. While every attempt has been made to verify the information shared in this publication, neither the author nor the affiliates assume any responsibility for errors, omissions or contrary interpretation of the subject matter herein. Any perceived slights to any specific person(s) or organization(s) are purely unintentional. We have no control over the nature, content and availability of the web sites listed in this book. The inclusion of any web site links does not necessarily imply a recommendation or endorse the views expressed within them. Simon James takes no responsibility for, and will not be liable for, the websites being temporarily unavailable or being removed from the internet. The accuracy and completeness of information provided herein and opinions stated herein are not guaranteed or warranted to produce any particular results, and the advice and strategies contained herein may not be suitable for every individual. The author shall not be liable for any loss incurred as a consequence of the use and application, directly or indirectly, of any information presented in this work. This publication is designed to provide information in regard to the subject matter covered. Neither the author nor the publisher assume any responsibility for any errors or omissions, nor do they represent or warrant that the ideas, information, actions, plans, suggestions contained in this book are in all cases accurate. It is the reader's responsibility to find advice before putting anything written in this book into practice. The information in this book is not intended to serve as legal advice.

Table of Contents

Acknowledgements v

Foreword 1

1. Why Train Your Cockapoo 3

    Equipment 3

    Training Environment 4

2. Canine psychology 5

    Learn how your dog learns 5

3. How to train your Cockapoo 7

4. Teach your Cockapoo his name 9

5. House training 11

    How to toilet train your puppy 11

6. Crating 13

7. Basic Commands 17

    Sit 17

    Down 19

    Stay 21

    Walking on the lead 23

    Come 25

8. Correcting bad behaviours 29

    What makes for a happy Cockapoo 29

    Pulling on lead 30

    Problem Barking..31

    Solutions 32

    Train him not to bark 32

    Overcoming separation anxiety 33

    Jumping up 34

9. First Tricks 35

    Shake a Paw...35

    Roll Over 36

10. Training Classes..37

11. Wrap up 39

    Top Tips for teaching and training:................................39

Acknowledgements

Thanks to Alan, Rob, Sue and Karen for researching and contributing their knowledge to this project.

About the Author

Simon James is a dog lover pure and simple. He has owned and trained many dogs, and cross-breeds. The simple, four-step method used in this guide, is inspired by the Dogs Trust Training Course and working with Labradoodle owners.

This book has been adapted thoughtfully to the Labradoodle breed for two reasons. Firstly, because there is too much 'bad training' advice and 'general training' advice that dog owners follow. Secondly, as a response to the growing numbers of unwanted Labradoodles that are entered into dog shelters every year. This situation is heart-breaking for any dog lover, so your donation will be given to Many Tears Animal Rescue (MTAR) as a result of you purchasing this book.

Simon consulted with other Cockapoo owners whilst writing this book.

Foreword

This is a book for Cockapoo owners although the training techniques could be used to train any dog. Cockapoo's are known to respond well to training and particularly to positive rewards based training like the system explained in this book.

Bringing a new dog home, particularly a puppy, is a day full of excitement for the new owner and full of high expectations about a new fun-filled life together. All the imagined good times can quickly turn to frustration is however your daily walks turn into a daily battle of 'yank and yell' or you're stuck in the park as the sun sets unable to get him back on his leash.

Six weeks after bringing him home, a human canine relationship doesn't have to end in disappointment. But judging from the number of adolescent dogs in rescue centres sadly, this is sometimes not the case.

Unfortunately, some people's experiences of dog training are littered with punishment based techniques and aggressive dog handlers. This has led to many people being turned off from training and just finding their own way-and probably putting up with bad canine behaviour as their way of life.

Another reason for not pursuing training is laziness or lack of confidence on the part of the owner. This turns out to be a false economy in the long run, not least because an untrained dog just doesn't come back when called.

Want I want you to really believe is that dog training can be 100% successful and enjoyable for dog and owner. That you can both be partners and companions so you're new Cockapoo becomes a respected and respectful member of his new family.

Read on and I'll show you how!

1. Why Train Your Cockapoo

A well-trained dog is a joy to live with. You don't have to worry when someone visits or if there are children around. You can just relax and enjoy your time together.

Your Cockapoo will be excited about almost any outing you can imagine. So, having a well-trained Cockapoo will allow him all the freedom he craves. You can take him everywhere with you, to visit friends, to the park, to the pub even to work, because you know he will be well behaved.

It's not just about freedom though- it's also about safety. You owe it to your dog to keep him safe, well behaved and appropriate in what he does. And also, to ensure anyone that comes into contact with your Cockapoo is safe.

A well-trained Cockapoo is a happy Cockapoo and having him well trained will make you a happy and proud owner.

Equipment

What do you need to train your dog? It's actually quite a minimal outlay that anyone can afford:

- A collar with a buckle and an identity collar. Try and find a collar that is wide as possible so it's comfortable for him
- A normal lead
- A training lead 6ft with a clip on both ends
- Treats: Lots of healthy treats that your dog loves, chopped up small to about the size of your little finger nail. Cheese,

sausage, chicken--whatever he will be prepared to work hard for

Training Environment

To start with you will need a quiet indoor space, free from distractions so you dog can focus on you. And of course, your Cockapoo! I hope you enjoy this fun, easy training program to transform your relationship with your dog

2. Canine psychology

When you bring a new dog into your home, particularly a puppy, nearly all his activities will be controlled. Most people get into trouble with puppies because they give them way too much freedom. Mayhem ensues and the 'fun puppy' experience soon turns sour.

That's why it's important to establish an early bond with your dog during training. As the programme develops over weeks and months your Cockapoo will gain your trust and you can entrust him with more and more freedom.

The Cockapoo is the perfect example of a dog that has become skilled at learning from and anticipating human behaviour. The Poodle is known to be one of the cleverest dogs on the planet. Also, the toy and miniature Cockapoo varieties have been bred as companion dogs. So you have a dog that wants to learn and wants to please- the job is half done!

Learn how your dog learns

As well as learning from his owner what is and isn't acceptable, your Cockapoo is also interacting and learning from the world around him. This is sometimes referred to by dog trainers as 'accidental learning'.

Dogs do what works for them. If they are rewarded by doing something they will do it again.

If your Cockapoo has a bad experience from doing something he will quickly learn to stop doing that thing.

If he doesn't get anything beneficial *or* bad from doing something he will gradually lose interest and stop.

With that in mind, canine psychology can be summed up in three ways:

1. Experience something good = will do more of
2. Experience something bad = will stop doing it
3. Experience something neither good nor bad = Gradually stop

Once you have learned that dogs will do repeatedly whatever they experience is good for them, you can use that to great advantage with your training programme.

A common misconception is that dogs respond to domination because of their original instincts learned from living in packs. This is the false thinking behind a lot of punishment based training programmes that thankfully, are far less prevalent than they were 20 years ago.

More recent research shows that wolves function in small family circle, usually led by parents, with no need for aggression to control behaviour. The bottom line is your dog will not seek to dominate you so there is no need to exert dominance over him. His natural instinct is to want to be part of a family that looks out for each other. Yes, they are used to working hard for food and are driven to that end. But as the head of the family, you control that resource and your dog will respect you because of it. You can also use it to shape your dog's behaviour. As a Cockapoo owner that means you can train him to fit in with your life and not the other way around.

3. How to train your Cockapoo

This book will show you a fun, effective way to train your Cockapoo.

The way to achieve this is with a positive, reward-based training program that rewards your dog when he does things right.

Positive still means you're building the essential boundaries your dog needs. But it will also build trust and a bond between you that will serve your life-relationship together so well.

Old fashioned training focused on what the dog was doing wrong then punishing that behaviour, like yanking back on the lead. This kind of aggression towards dogs is very much frowned upon and challenged by most dog trainers today.

Your challenge is to show your dog what you want him to do and reward him for it. Dogs love food they don't need to be taught they love food; t's always a positive experience for them. Dogs have always had to work hard to eat- it's an instinct. So, we are going to use that to our advantage.

Dogs always repeat things that are beneficial for them. Remember, If it's good for the dog he will do it again. A well-timed treat rewarding the desired behaviour is a guarantee it will keep happening.

Why don't we punish our dog? Simple. Punishment erodes the bond between you. Our dog is our companion and family member. We don't treat friends and family by hitting and shouting when they get something wrong. Dogs are thinking, feeling emotional creatures, just like us. So why should they do something unless we show them it's fun and beneficial for them.

Are treats bribes?

Some people will say that giving your dog treats is simply a bribe. To begin with it is, but you will reduce the treats and replace it with praise as your dog has more fun doing what he is enjoying being taught. So don't go looking for what he's doing wrong and start rewarding what he does right and have fun!

4. Teach your Cockapoo his name

Many people forget to teach their dog their name and what their name means.

You need to teach your Cockapoo something good is about to happen when his name is called. So he learns you (his owner) really is worth paying attention to. This is the best way to be able to get his attention when you need it and it's also the first step to getting your Cockapoo to come back when you call him.

This means you can call him away from things you don't want him to get involved in. Cockapoo's like any dog, can only think about one thing at a time. So, if they're thinking about you they can't think about anything else.

To start with:

1. Make sure you have plenty of treats on you
2. Wait for a time when you're relaxing at home and your dog is not paying attention to you
3. Then call his name (using a clear bright tone)
4. Wait until your Cockapoo looks at you and then give him a treat
5. If he doesn't look at you, don't repeat his name

There are no second chances with this one, if he doesn't respond he just doesn't get a treat. Just try again a few minutes later. You want him to look at you the first time.

4. Teach your Cockapoo his name

You can practice this anytime, in the park, in the bath, where ever. Once he learns to look at you when his name is called, he will associate his name with getting something yummy!

He soon learns his name means *he must* pay attention to *you*. This is a great start point to go on and teach him other things.

And remember, if he's not looking at you he's not listening.

5. House training

For those of you that are bringing a Cockapoo puppy home one of your immediate concerns is to get your puppy house trained.

Cockapoo's like all dogs naturally want to be clean and they do not want to urinate or defecate in their home, den or crate.

With toilet training you have to build a routine around your puppy's needs and these needs are consistently similar in all puppies. The reasons your Cockapoo may go to the toilet indoors are usually excitement; anxiety and stress about being left alone; plus, not been given the opportunity to go outside.

It's important you have patience and not over react when accidents happen as this will just add to your puppy's anxiety. This in turn slows the process of learning the correct way to relieve himself.

How to toilet train your puppy

No puppy is perfect and there will always be little accidents. Fortunately, Cockapoos are highly intelligent so this process is achievable in a matter of weeks, depending on how much effort you are prepared to put in.

The key to toilet training is giving the puppy *every* opportunity to do his business in the right place. This means you need to be available through the day to show him where he should be going to relieve himself. All Puppies have immature bladders so need to go regularly and should be taken outside:

5. House training

- At least every hour depending upon the puppy's age.
- After waking from a nap
- After every meal
- After any excitement, e.g. visitors to the home or playtime
- After a period of being left alone

Some may say it's easy to know when its naturally time for your dog to go to the toilet, but tell-tale signs are when he becomes fidgety, copiously sniffing around and beginning to circle before squatting.

You must accompany him every time he goes outside or to the garden. Try and go to the same place each time so he understands it's time, and take a treat to reward them.

Keep following this process diligently, and remember the golden rule is give your puppy as much opportunity as possible to go to the toilet and reward and praise your him when he goes in the correct place

As you will learn in the next chapter, crating is another helpful aid in toilet training your Cockapoo puppy.

6. Crating

What size crate?

Even the 'standard' or 'maxi' size Cockapoo doesn't grow to be a large dog, but your crate will have to be large enough for him to stand, sit, turn, stretch, lie down and spread out. It's important that the crate is well ventilated. Most are designed that way and there is a huge variety to choose from.

Creating a cosy den

Don't think because you are crate training your puppy you are caging him. A dog crate serves several important functions for a puppy if introduced properly into his routine. It will become a place of comfort and safety and help your puppy get used to confined spaces. And very useful in the early days when he needs transporting for trips out the house or to the vets.

Place the crate in an area away from the family hubbub but not too far away so he still feels the comfort of having you close by. Here a few things that will transform the crate from being a sterile environment to a place your little Cockapoo enjoys returning to:

1. Be sure to make it a positive experience
2. Gradually introduce him to his new safe place
3. Be patient. Learning to trust the crate as his new den happens slowly

The process

6. Crating

There are three important points to remember about crate training:

1. Again, be sure to make it a positive experience
2. Be patient as learning to trust the crate as his new den happens slowly
3. Gradually introduce him to his new safe place

Step one - introduction to the crate

To begin, place the crate in an area that your puppy is used to but slightly out the way, like your living room or kitchen and leave the door open so he can come and go.

Tempt you puppy into the crate by putting some treats or chews in there. Your puppy should soon associate the crate as being a happy place where he enjoys snacks and plays with toys. If he is apprehensive be encouraging with you voice and gradually move him closer by serving up treats and petting him right next to the entrance. Soon he will find his way in there and settle.

This step may take several days so be patient and don't force the issue.

Step Two

Once your puppy has accepted the crate you can begin to serve meals in there. And once he is safely in and enjoying his meal close the door.

Open the door again when he is finished but begin to leave the door closed a little longer each time. This will lead him to naturally rest after eating and have his first crate sleep time. If your puppy starts whining or barking or exhibiting any signs of distress you may have over done it with the amount of time spent with the door closed.

Once step two is complete your puppy's crate has become his den. A safe comfortable place to eat, rest and relax.

Step three - going out of sight

Once your puppy has started to trust his new environment you can begin to leave him for short periods. Just make sure when you do leave, your Cockapoo is happy with a chew stick or favourite toy and has water to drink.

TIP - Buy an activity feeder, like the popular *Kong* and stuff it with food mix (cheese mixed with peanut butter and crumbled dog biscuits are a popular choice) so he is happy and has plenty to chew on.

If he is struggling with being in the crate alone just sit next to him quietly for a few minutes until he is engaged with his activity feeder and then slip out the room. Return in a few minutes and just sit quietly. Repeat this routine until your puppy is comfortable being alone.

Practicing this step in the day and evening is also a good idea.

Making sure your puppy is occupied in the crate is key when he is getting used to the new environment because you don't want him to get bored or anxious and start barking. It's easy to fall into the trap of giving into this behaviour by letting him out. But then you are just reinforcing him barking.

Wait until there is even a momentary break in his behaviour *then* let him out. Like all training, timing is everything!

Step four - moving on

You will have successful completed step three when your puppy can be left alone inside the crate for about 30 minutes to enjoy treats. Make your re-appearance is as low-key as possible so as not to create excitement.

Closing thoughts on crating

You never use the crate to lock your dog away for long periods while you are off doing something else— that's not its function and using it in this way is completely inappropriate. A period of time up to three hours is okay, but beyond that time frame you're not being sensitive to your dog's needs.

Also, puppies have immature bladders and bowels and cannot hold themselves for very long. It's quite traumatic for a dog to mess inside its crate as it goes strongly against their natural instincts. Leaving any dog alone to the point they are desperate to relieve themselves is cruel.

If used right, the crate is a place of peace and security that gravitates the puppy to naturally find some down time and rest.

7. Basic Commands

Sit

This is a great first exercise as it's something your Cockapoo does naturally anyway. It's the start of good canine manners. A dog that is sitting quietly isn't jumping on anyone.

Once you have mastered the four simple steps to teach him to sit you can use these steps to progress further and the sky's the limit!

Lure your dog

The first step is always to show your dog what you want him to do.

1. Take a treat
2. Hold it on the end of his nose
3. Then lift it back, and over, his head
4. As his head comes up, his bottom has to come down
5. And then he gets the treat

Practice this a lot. It may take hours or weeks. But what you want, is your dog to sit as soon as your hand comes up.

Make your dog think

The next thing you want to teach your Cockapoo is for him to work out- *what was it that got me the treat last time?* You want him to think, *if I put my bottom on the floor I get a treat!*

So, put a treat on the end of the nose, then bring the treat up to your chest and establish eye contact. Your dog should sit and wait expectantly. When he looks at you in the seated position give him the treat. You need to repeat this lots until he really gets the hang of it. As soon as he sees the treat you want his bottom to go down.

Name the action

Only start this step when you are positive when he sees the treat his bottom will go down. If that's the case, now is time to slip in the command.

Remember timing is everything with commands. Just as his bottom is touching the floor, say 'Sit' in a strong voice. Your Cockapoo will soon associate the command word with putting his bottom on the floor.

Practice everywhere

This is a key element of dog training. Now it's time to get out there in every location you can think of.

Start in a place where there are few distractions until he gets really good at offering the sit position. Then practice in more busy places. Keep him guessing when the treat is going to come so he *really* has to work for the treat.

Start reducing treats and praising him instead. Eventually he will always sit when you give the command wherever you are.

Phew, how reassuring is that to know you have that obedience from your dog when you really need it!

Now that your Cockapoo understands 'sit', he's half way there to lying down. Having him lie quietly beside you is very useful in so many situations.

Before you start, make sure you have yummy treats and a spacious enclosed area.

Step one - As before, lure the dog into the position you want.

1. Starting from the sit position, put the treat in your closed hand
2. Place your hand directly in front of your dog's nose
3. Move your hand straight down
4. Your dog should lie down

TIPS:

- Don't get tempted to push your dog as he will resist you. Just lure him down with the treat.
- Don't lure him down in a forward motion. He probably will walk forward and just wander off.
- Practise repeatedly, everywhere not just at home

Make your dog think

Take your treat, show your dog you have got it and wait. And wait for long enough that he begins to think, *now what was it that got me the treat last time? Oh yes, it was that lying down thing that got me my sausage!*

Practice this until he lies down straight away. Make sure you are quick to give the treat just as he lies down. Remember you're not rewarding him for getting back up again!

When your Cockapoo starts to get good at this it ends up very simple.

You show the treat... dog lies down...and the treat is given immediately dog offers down position.

Name the Action

Once you are certain your dog has accepted what he should be doing, it's time to link the behaviour to the command word.

Again, it's important that you say the word *precisely* at the time the dog hits the floor. This establishes the link in his mind to build the connection between the command word and the down behaviour he's offering.

Practice Everywhere

Now you are confident your dog knows the command 'Down' in the house it's time to take it outside.

Start somewhere there are few distractions, like your garden or a quiet area of the park. Gradually build up the routine in more busy places where there are other people and dogs.

You will need your 6ft training leash to clip to your belt so you've got your hands free to work the treats.

Stay

This is the beginning of having a go-anywhere-dog. You can teach your dog to stay in either a stand, sit or down. Very useful when attaching a leash, or popping into the shops.

The down-stay

Make sure your dog really knows the down well before teaching the down- stay.

1. Command your dog into the down position
2. Hold out your hand, palm up as though it's a stop sign
3. Count to five
4. And then quickly move forward and reward your dog by giving the treat

Make sure your Cockapoo is not getting up as you give the treat. Again, it's important he does not build a connection between getting up and receiving a treat.

Build this up so your poo can stay down for 30 seconds. If he moves blame that on yourself and get him back in position. You need to be really patient. Then move the teaching to different locations.

Creating distance

Put your dog in the down position with treat in hand. Then take a step back. If he stays, step back to him immediately and give him the treat.

Summary

Dogs do find this hard. Build up the distance gradually. Move at your dog's speed. Get out and about and practice everywhere, starting with no distractions in a safe secure area.

And until he is reliable with the stay command use your 6ft training lead.

Walking on the lead

Your goal here is for your Cockapoo to walk nicely on the lead without pulling. This will transform your walk and make it safer and more fun.

To start with don't bring a lead. This isn't a tug of war- we just want to model the right behaviour for your dog to learn.

Step one - show the dog what you want him to do

7. Basic Commands

- Take a treat and hold it in front of his nose so he can see where it is and just take a few steps forward
- Your dog will follow you
- If your dog is losing interest put the treat back on his nose
- Soon your dog will be walking beside you
- Remember to give him the treat after he manages about 10 steps
- Start building up the distance before he gets the treat

Step 2 - Make your dog think

As before you want your dog to start connecting the walking behaviour with getting a treat.

- Let your dog have a good sniff of the treat in your hand
- Then take the treat off his nose and begin walking slowly
- Your dog will follow, walking by your side
- After 10 or 15 paces give him the treat
- Increase the distance before he gets the treat
- Practice this a lot so every time you move he walks beside you.

Step 3 - Name the command

Now you're going to insert the command word as your dog begins to walk beside you. This can be *heel* or *close* whatever you want.

- I recommend establishing eye contact with your dog while they are in the sit position.
- Then say 'heel' and move forward
- As you begin to practice this try and keep eye contact

- Once your dog has stayed by your side as you walk forward for a meaningful amount of time you can give the treat and make a fuss of him.

Step 4 - Practise everywhere.

And be patient.
To train 'the recall' you will need a 6ft training lead.

This lead is long enough that you can get a good distance from your Cockapoo but you will still keep him safe on lead. It should have a clip on each end to attach to you and your Cockapoo.

Lure you dog

As usual, you want to show your dog what you want him to do and lure him with the treat.

1. Get your dog's favourite treat
2. Put the treat right on the end of his nose
3. Now walk backwards - and your dog will follow. This is teaching your dog to follow
4. Once he's followed you backwards for about 10 seconds give him the treat and stop

Practice this a lot so your dog really *knows* he should be following you when you go backwards. Some Cockapoos learn this in a few sessions while others take a few weeks. It's important to understand you must go at *your* dog's pace and not get frustrated.

Make your dog think

Step 2 is to make your dog offer the same behaviour but without the treat.

7. Basic Commands

1. Adopt the same pose as before and put your closed hand next to your dog's nose
2. Now walk backwards- and your dog will follow
3. Make a huge fuss of your dog when he completes the right behaviour so the praise becomes the reward.

Be really fun and exuberant while doing this exercise and don't worry about feeling silly.

Name the Action

Once your dog has learned to follow you, put a name to what you have just taught.

Use your dog's name to get his attention. *Remember, if a dog is not looking at you he's not listening to you.* After you have said his name encourage him to come to you as you did before.

As he starts to offer the behaviour put the word in- *So he links coming to you with that word.* It's always name first, then the command (which is usually 'come') but it could be anything. When he offers the behaviour, you want to give a treat and praise.

Once he starts doing this you can practice anywhere. You can play a game called 'ping pong puppy'. This is when you and a friend take turns calling his name

TIP: have big open body language, arms wide. If you lean forward you are encouraging them to go away.

Recap

1. Say his name
2. Say Come
3. When he comes to you give the treat

Outside / off leash

Make sure you're in a really safe environment like a large field, or enclosed space. A place where nothing bad can happen to your Cockapoo if he doesn't come back.

Make sure you have your dog's attention.

Be really enthused, over exaggerated when calling him back to you. This makes it fun for your dog. Make sure he will always return to you 100% of the time before letting him off the leash in an unsafe location.

8. Correcting bad behaviours

What makes for a happy Cockapoo

Many people take a dog into their lives without really understanding how they can ensure they are healthy and happy and also how they can make them easy to live with.

Exercise is the number one thing you can do that will improve nearly all behavioural problems. A dog as inquisitive as the Cockapoo is easily bored, and stores pent up energy or can often feel frustration.

Cockapoos need exercising every single day. Depending on what type of Cockapoo you have (Working or Show Cocker origin) that may mean half an hour exercise a day, or a couple of hours several times a day, with lots of running and play off lead to keep him happy.

Over the years people have bred dogs for specific jobs. Depending on what those jobs are determine what that dog is going to be like to live with. Some dogs are bred for retrieving or working or as lap dogs. Exercise is so important for making sure you dog is happy. Particularly dogs from a 'Working' stock that need loads of exercise if they are truly going to be happy. How much time you have to devote to exercising your dog is your main consideration when you decide what type of dog you are going to get.

But it's not all about physical exercise. Dogs need to use their brains. Training is good for that. It's a great way to bond with your dog and keep him mentally healthy. There are lots of interactive toys that can help with separation anxiety or just to keep him mentally engaged. It can be as simple as a *Kong* toy with some treats stuffed inside or something more complex like puzzles to keep them occupied.

To be happy your Cockapoo needs:

- Good food
- Mental stimulation
- Your company (because dogs are social creatures)
- And plenty of exercise

Dogs need your energy and time so go out and have fun with your dog! If your Cockapoo is getting the correct amount of exercise, training him will be much easier.

Pulling on lead

Step one - Use your 6ft training lead and a flat loose collar and some treats. Find a quiet place with no distractions.

The objective is to teach him that a loose lead is good. He has to know the minute the lead goes on, it *has* to be loose.

- Walk around (it doesn't matter which side he is on) and when the lead is loose give him a treat
- If the lead gets tight, stop and stand- he doesn't get a treat.
- This takes practice

- It doesn't matter where he is, if the leads' loose he gets the treat

Step two - Add a distraction

Put his favourite toy about 20 paces away. Only allow him to walk to the toy when the lead is loose. As soon as he pulls on the lead stop and stand. And wait. When the lead goes loose again walk forward with him until he reaches the toy.

It does take a lot of commitment. If he pulls just once and he gets to where he wants faster the work becomes un-done. He has to believe with all his heart and soul that the fastest way to get there is on a loose lead.

If you are having days where you know you don't have the commitment or the time then put him in a harness. It's far better that you control him on a walk with a harness then let him half strangle himself in a collar.

Problem Barking

The first thing to remember is that dogs bark for a reason:

- Barking at the edge of his territory - when he sees the postman or another dog

- Boredom barkers - dogs that are craving companionship or mental stimulation

- Some breeds just bark more than others

Solutions

This one is relatively simple to cure. Use baby-gates and crating or put him somewhere he can't see passers-by.

Boredom barkers

Firstly, make sure they have been exercised. A well exercised dog will bark less. If you're going to be out for long periods then ask a friend or dog walker to stop by even if it's just to play a game with him. Dogs are really social animals and generally don't do well on their own. Barking is just a symptom of this.

You can also give them something to occupy him (like a Kong stuffed with treats). This will make your leaving, beneficial to him, and stop the *I'm on my own now*, barking.

Train him not to bark

1. When your dog is barking join in with him (let yourself go and don't be embarrassed just have fun). You can even add a command to it like 'woof'

2. Then take a treat out and hold it in front of his nose

3. He will stop barking because he has to...and just wait

4. After 5 seconds give him the treat

5. Repeat and extend the waiting period

This will reinforce to him that not barking equals something good will happen. Like all these training sessions it takes time and patience. But if you're having fun it's no trouble at all.

Overcoming separation anxiety

There are many dogs that are so attached to their owner they can't stand to be on their own. A Cockapoo is known to suffer from separation anxiety particularly as the smaller breeds have been bred as companion dogs.

It's emotionally difficult for you the owner and even worse for the dog. In fact, it's just total panic for a dog that has never been taught to cope on his own.

Your prevention of separation anxiety needs to start the moment you first bring him home as a puppy or adult dog. This lesson will actually teach him to look forward to the time he is by himself.

1. First of all, get some baby-gates installed around your house

2. Give your Cockapoo something really nice to chew (the *Kong* for example stuffed with treats) and leave him to it

3. Leave via the baby gate and allow him to enjoy his reward

4. To start with go to the end of the garden or around the block

5. Keep doing this each day and increase the time you are away

By gradually leaving him alone with something tasty for him you're teaching him the coping strategies to stay on his own and he is learning 'alone time' is normal and part of his routine. Teaching this is going to save you both so much anxiety and stress- it's essential training for the Cockapoo.

Jumping up

This is an easy behaviour to correct but first, it's important to understand why your dog jumps up to greet you and others. For dogs, the natural way to greet another dog is to lick around their mouths the same way a puppy does with its mother.

So, while you think your muddy, scratchy dog is rude for jumping up, he thinks he is greeting you appropriately and politely. So we need to change the way he thinks.

All you're going to do is reward the behaviour you want. And teach him the only way he will get your attention is when all four of his feet are on the ground.

Step one- When your dog jumps up just ignore him. Cross your arms in front of you and look away. Eventually he will sit down. The moment he does assume the sit position give him the treat. Straight away he learns if he wants a treat, his feet must be on the floor.

Step two - Practice with every member of your family, children, granny, everyone.

8. Correcting bad behaviours

9. First Tricks

Some people think that teaching tricks is demeaning to them. This is not true. You and your Cockapoo having fun together is what your dog really craves. It enhances the bond between you and also keeps your dog mentally engaged which is very important for this breed in particular as they are so mentally agile.

If your Cockapoo is less than six months old when you begin teaching tricks, keep your training sessions short (about three minutes) and make the sessions lots of fun. As your Cockapoo becomes an adult, you can extend your sessions, because they will be able to maintain their focus for longer.

As always, find a place where there are no distractions and make sure your Cockapoo is giving you his full attention. Holding eye contact demonstrates you have his attention.

Shake a Paw

This is one of the easiest tricks to teach your Cockapoo. Practice every day until they are 100% reliable with this trick, and then it will be time to add another trick to his repertoire.

Most dogs are naturally right or left pawed. If you want to know which paw your Cockapoo favours, ask him to shake his paw.

Find a quiet place to practice, without noisy distractions or other pets, and stand or sit in front of him.

1. Place him in the sitting position and hold a treat in your left hand.

2. Say the command "Shake" while putting your right hand behind his left or right paw and pulling the paw gently

toward yourself until you are holding his paw in your hand.

3. Take it turns with right then left and you will see he favours one paw or another.

4. Immediately praise him and give the treat.

Most dogs will learn the "Shake" trick very quickly.

Roll Over

You will find that just like your Cockapoo is naturally either right or left pawed, that they will also naturally want to roll either to the right or the left side. Take advantage of this by asking your dog to roll to the side they naturally prefer.

1. Sit with your dog on the floor and put them in the down position.

2. Hold a treat in your hand and place it close to their nose with a closed hand. While they are in the lying position, move the treat to the right or left side of their head so that they have to roll over to get it.

3. You will quickly see which side they naturally want to roll to; once you notice this, practice holding the treat to that side of his head.

4. Once they roll over to that side, immediately give him the treat and praise him.

You can say the verbal cue "Over" while you demonstrate the hand signal motion (moving your right hand in a half circular motion) from one side of his head to the other.

10. Training Classes

If you need more hands-on support, or the camaraderie of other dog owners you should think about attending an organised training club.

Having the insight and skills of a professional trainer and classmates can be very valuable, with the additional benefit of socialising your dog under controlled, safe conditions.

There are a range of classes to choose from: puppy classes; competitive obedience or fly ball— one will suit you and your Cockapoo's interests and needs.

A good club should:

- Be in a spacious communal place that offers safety for both dog and owner
- Have small class sizes so the instructor can supervise all dogs at all times and be able to give all individuals adequate attention
- Have appropriate class levels for different skill levels
- Make sure all dogs are under control at all times
- Be run in a friendly and professional manner
- Not allow shouting at dogs or owners but instead encourage all to have fun!
- Not use choke or 'check' chains but rather ensure dogs wear flat collars for training
- Never use or teach physical punishment for any reason

The best way to search for a training club is word of mouth, local vet clinics and rescue organisations usually keep lists of local classes, although these will probably not be recommendations so check them out first.

The Kennel Club and the Association of Pet Dog Trainers (APDT) should be able to recommend a club in your area or write to:

Association of Pet Dog Trainers
PO Box 17,
Kempsford,
GL7 4WZ
Tel: 01285 810811
www.apdt.co.uk

All APDT members use methods which are kind, fair and effective and must adhere to a strict code of practice.

11. Wrap up

Top Tips for teaching and training:

I hope you are having fun training your Cockapoo with this fun, positive reward based system. Just be patient and stay committed to the process of your Cockapoo learning. It's also about you the owner learning to be an effective trainer and that means you have to stay focused. Once you see results and benefit from having a well-trained Cockapoo, my guess is you won't want to stop.

Here are some final quick tips to keep you on the right track.

Remember

- ❖ Training should be FUN for both dog and owner

- ❖ Training should always be based on POSITIVE rewards

- ❖ NEVER punish your dog – this will cause him to be frightened of you

- ❖ SHOW your dog what you are trying to teach him

- ❖ NEVER physically force him into a position

- ❖ Train at your Cockapoos pace (some dogs take longer than others)

- ❖ Be patient and keep your commands consistent

- ❖ Don't let him get bored, keep training sessions short

- ❖ Never 'train' in a busy area, only begin to build up the distractions gradually once he knows the commands really well

Reviews And Other Books

If you have enjoyed this book please leave an honest review. The more books sold the more I donate MTAR- so please submit a review today. For in depth feedback and suggestions to improve the book please email cockapooebooks@gmail.com. Future editions will be sent to you when released.

Want more Cockapoo Guides?

50% off Cockapoo Bundle using this coupon code at check-out: **50OFF**

Printed in Great Britain
by Amazon